Create A New Idea

Author's Biography

Abderrahmane Dakir was born in Casablanca in Morocco. Since graduating from University Hassan II

he has worked in international companies since 1998 as Web Engineer. In 2003, he founded and now manages his own company 1NEWLOG.

Since January 2015, he started writing short-stories in English in order to share his ideas about life, family, nature with the rest of the world.

Preface

Mr. Dakir Abderrahmane talks about innovation as a
means to success. Eliciting answers to deep questions as
to the reasons for human existence and our constant
need to and ability to never give up. Perseverance and
strength in individuals and in teams, we forge our way
through history to create for the future though we only
focus on the present. "Creativity and harmony are keys to
our link with our own creator, since we take on many of
His attributes. He helps us to succeed." Mr Dakir.

I hope you enjoy reading it as much as Mr. Dakir enjoyed
writing it for you.

Sonia Cooke
English teacher native speaker

Can companies continue to succeed for many years without innovating?

Can people develop a new lifestyle just by thinking about a new idea?

Each day we expect to live new and varied experiences. We need to know what today's weather will be, we need to read something new, listen to something new, watch a new video, touch a new object, smell a new perfume to increasingly improve our lifestyles. So we should subject ourselves to a kind of daily innovation in order to feel this change every day.

When I was a student, I hoped to work in the field where I could continually practice and experiment with new things as a researcher; spending all my time learning cutting edge things.

After my graduation, I worked in a software company where I gained experience and learned many tricks. I remembered that I accepted a position in one company even though they gave me a half the salary that I was given in another company. I appreciated it just to be able to use the newest IT.

Later I founded my company so that I could work in a calmer environment since the most important thing for me is not earning as much money and possible and working like a machine, but enjoying learning about the latest ideas and applying them in the smartest way within our customer's projects.

My hope is to become a big geek in this field by working from this great passion I have for it. I have been focused on learning the newest computer language and working with a tremendous team in order to share the point of each and every detail.

The team I mentioned are all extraverts and as a result we create a buzzing atmosphere with lots of energy when we work together to search for an answer for each trick or problem. Each project is a challenge for us; we have to make a difference, we have to create a new design for each website. So, each person has to give a new idea about the purpose of any given project.

The more we develop the project; the eager we are to improve it in the best possible way. Finally, we are proud to create any project that can help any person or company in our society, especially in terms of healthcare in hospitals, schools, industry, fashion as our traditional woman clothes as Caftan, decoration in hotels, restaurant, houses, government building, ..., etc.

I owe all this success to all members of the team that work together to achieve these projects.

Even though sometimes things get stressful when we are meeting deadlines for applications; we put a strategy in place to reach our goal, step by step. We don't see failure as failure, but we see a failure as a chance to fix it and make it better.

I consider the company where we work to be a mindful place since we feel free from worry and thought, free from the past and the future, we fully engage ourselves in the now, to be in the zone or a fluid state to do our work at our best.

We work in a café. Firstly, because we have our second breakfast there all together but also because it leads us to focus more on our business.

Remember, cafés have historically been places to discuss and learn new ideas, hence why so many artists, writers and thinkers have created the best of their work in cafés. Beethoven and Bach wrote much of their music in a café. According to new research, the background noise of café can make you think more creatively.

By creating a new idea, we can change the world like the great inventions of Nikola Tesla who opened the door to the modern world with his incredible inventions, especially AC power and Thomas Edison who invented the light bulb, it took him many years, he made over a thousand attempts before he found the solution in the bamboo plant in Japan. He understood that failure is just a part of success.

Without them, we might still be living in a world of darkness. I don't need to tell you how they worked hard to achieve their goals.

So experience and challenge are all things we need to make the creativity flourish.

For those inventors and creators of a new idea I write this:

Their dream lights the world,
Their vision warms the cold.

They spent all their life in event,
Their system is safe and efficient.

Without them, I live still in the darkness,
Their idea leads me to the light.

They open the door to the modern world,
Their achievements are worth more than gold.

They don't care about money,
Having quality time is their honey.

Their war is protecting themselves from businesses,
Their peace is thinking in loneliness.

Their refuge is discovering new knowledge,
Their invention speaks the best language.

We can apply the creativity of a new idea not only into physical structures but also into services like service restaurant. Café, Hotel, sport, art, and any else field.

I'd like to mention at this point, a successful business in the food field, McDonalds, that gives us delicious ice cream. I'm astounded by the people who work for this company how they are organized to deliver us food in the best way.

I'd also like to mention the Google engine that provides us the best service to share ideas. They invest over twenty percent of their time in research to be leaders in innovation.

In my great country, Morocco, that I'm proud of I prefer talking about people who have started their businesses from scratch, as of the great Caterer Rahal in the restaurant field who export his knowledge in the world.

Miloud Chaabi, in the constructer field, who also expanded his business to an international level. They worked so hard and when they died they left behind workforces of over twenty thousand people in their huge companies.

Not forgetting other names like Hassan for the tea distribution, Akhenouch for gas distribution ….and others. All we need is reminding of their strongest effort to participate in the development of human resources in many countries.

I want to show you how a person who thinks about his idea is not only a productive person, but also he can be responsible for hiring over thousands of people and in return be responsible for reducing the rate of unemployment.

Creating a new idea makes everyone happy and allows them to follow their dreams. It's another way to live in love and in peace since we should be leaving behind a message that makes us different from other creatures.

I'd like to end with this thought: we all need God's light to help us to do our best. He creates everything from nothing. Creation only comes from the natural source.

For a new idea we need to use our brain that was created by Him to try to make something beneficial for human beings. We should embed our creator's attributes within us to be creative, in order to offer up our best work.

Work, which develops in harmony with our beautiful natural environment and which has the ability to help us to enjoy ourselves more, whilst being involved in this magical universe.

I sum up the creativity of a new idea in this short poem:

Failure is a chance to attempt,
From your birth to your death.

The greatest people of all time have succeeded,
Though how many times had they failed,
No one gave up or was discouraged.

Trying over and over again is a key,
To improve your plan and strategy.

Believing strongly your idea is a way,
To achieve your goal the next day.

Failure as a learning experience is better,
To persevere in your field or your career.

With time, you will be like a light,
In your lifetime or after your death.

www.ingramcontent.com/pod-product-compliance
Lightning Source LLC
Chambersburg PA
CBHW072023290526
45787CB00014B/1848